CW00382447

# In the Spaces Between the Shadows

LAURA HARRISON

TO / Kath

I hope you like the book

Love,
Laura

Copyright © 2020 Laura Harrison

All rights reserved.

ISBN: 9798608401268

Independently Published

# DEDICATION

I dedicate this book to Stephanie Forrest, for being my free therapist throughout everything these poems are about and for making me believe in myself when I didn't think it was possible.

# CONTENTS

## ACKNOWLEDGMENTS

Thank you to everyone who inspired the contents of this book. Whether I only met you briefly, or whether you played a huge part in my life, these poems wouldn't exist without you.

Thank you to my mum and dad for allowing me the freedom to do and be whatever I want, as long as it makes me happy.

Thank you to anyone who has ever read my poems. Whether you liked them or not, thank you for giving them a chance.

Thank you to my friends Kasia, Alex, Stephanie and Claire who believe in me and always have my back. You all make the world a better place and I am so glad that I have you in my life.

# ALL THAT I AM LIVING FOR

I know that I am difficult to handle at times
but you are so good at reading between the lines
so please don't ever lose that ability
because you are the only person who understands me

I don't know who to be without you around
so please don't leave me lying on the ground
for this past year you have been all that I know
how will I cope if you ever go

You are everything that I am scared to lose
so please don't ever leave any signs or clues
that you are about to walk out that door
and take away all that I am living for

# IS THAT ALL THERE IS TO LIFE

You are born, life sucks and then you die
is that all there is to life
you do the same thing every single day
just for death to come and take it all away

Go to school, go to college, get a job
keep on working until life stops
find the perfect home and the perfect man
just do whatever society tells you that you can

Ignore the rules, do what you like
don't let anyone tell you how to live your life
do everything you've always wanted to do
live your dream before it's taken away from you

## FOOL IN LOVE

I swore to myself that I would never be
the kind of girl who got back with a ex
yet here I am, packing my bags
after the second failed attempt.

I guess there's something addicting about you
that makes me come running back for more
but it's a known fact that addictions are dangerous
I should have known what was in store.

I wish that I could rip my heart out and destroy it
because I am sick of being in love with you
and I've been told that that we always hurt
the ones we love the most
so at least I know that you love me too.

# I FIND BEAUTY IN THE LITTLE THINGS

I find beauty in the little things
like a smile from a stranger
and all the resurrected flowers
on the first day of spring
watching the sunset with the person I love
and finding money I didn't know I had
the smell of a book
old or new
and doing something I didn't think I could do
the discovery of a song
I end up playing on repeat
and the feeling of warm grass underneath my bare feet
staying in bed whilst it's raining inside
and feeling better when I've had a little cry
playing a game that I loved as a kid
and a change in my routine that is unexpected.

I am so tiny in a world that is big
but I find it so hard to find beauty in me.

# LET ME TREAT YOU LIKE A BOOK

Let me treat you like a book
I want to read you from beginning to end
to discover the story that lies within you.
I want to sit with you besides a burning fire
with a cup of hot chocolate while it's raining outside
allow me to breathe in your beautiful scent
and stroke your spine with my fingertips.
I want to take care of you
to make sure that you never get damaged
or gather dust in your heart.
I want to be the person who will never tire of you
and I want to carry you with me wherever I go.
Let me treat you like a book
because you know that I would never do anything
to hurt one of those.

# IT WOULD BE EASIER IF YOU WERE DEAD

I can't stop myself from thinking
that it would be easier if you had died
because at least then you wouldn't have left me by choice
and it pains me knowing that I could just dial your number
or knock on your door
but I wouldn't even know how to talk to you anymore.
Things can never be the same
as they were when we were kids
discussing bands and the most recent boy you had kissed
I could ask you why you suddenly decided
that you don't want to know mc anymore
but my breath has already been wasted
on questions like that before
and I'm done with sitting around, waiting for you to come back
like a lost puppy that's been left in the park
I have a life to live
and I'm not going to waste it because of this
all that I can do is pretend you don't exist.

# ROUGH DRAFT

There are days when I find myself
surrounded by crumpled pieces of paper
that are inked with the thoughts and feelings
of my weary and troubled mind
crumpled, because the words that appear on them
aren't quite right
but my favourite thing about writing poetry
is that if I don't like the rough draft
I can change it
I can give the poem a whole new meaning
or I can start it all over again.

Life isn't that kind
we are born into a world
that demands perfection
we have to teach ourselves how to hope
that we will get it right on the first try
and if we don't
we have to learn how to walk whichever path
we happen to find ourselves on
and hope that somewhere along our perilous journey
we will be offered a new beginning
a blank page
that allows us to take that rough draft from the past
and re-write it.

# SAME SUBJECT, DIFFERENT POEM

Memories and thoughts of you
have been sprawled across the pages of my notebook
so many times
that it's a wonder I have any material left
but I have been told
never to bottle up my thoughts and feelings
and you have been at the forefront of my mind
ever since the day you walked out of my life
so I decided to let the ink bleed dry
rather than myself
and if anybody asks
I don't even think about you anymore
but me and my poetry know that's a lie
because I can't spend my entire life
with someone I thought was my hero
and forget them as quickly as they forgot me.
I have been dealing with words and metaphors
for the past three years now
I know how to disguise my emotions by what I say
but my poetry reflects what's happening in my mind
my poetry tells what I'm really feeling
when my mouth can't.

# THE SKIN I'M IN

Two steps through the classroom door
now I don't want to be here anymore
I feel their words pierce my heart like a knife
but I am still alive on the outside.
My feet feel heavy as I take a seat
it feels like a thousand eyes are following me
watching me to see if I break
but they won't be getting that satisfaction today.
I'm going to keep my head held high
and ignore the thoughts that they've placed in my mind
I'm going to be nice and smile right at them
because I've always been taught to
'kill them with kindness.'
Sometimes I feel like giving up
but my road to recovery has just begun
and I don't care if the perfect body is thin
I'm going to love the skin I'm in.

# WE'RE IN THIS TOGETHER

I'm not quite sure how the world works
all I know for certain
is that sometimes life hurts
but every stomach fluttering kiss
every dance in the moonlight
every wrong that feels so right
is worth it
my God, is it worth it.
so get out of bed
no excuses
let go of all the reasons why you're hurting
make yourself believe that today is the day
the day you stop wasting your life away.
I know it's not easy
nothing ever is
but trust me when I say
that there's more to life than this
so don't let your fears consume you
because what if I told you that I'm afraid too
what if I told you that we're the same
that I have had whole years that were not okay
but I am going to start living my life
despite the familiar fear taking over on the inside
it's been drilled into our brains
that no-one lives forever
and it's finally sinking in
that I'm nowhere near ready to die
so take my hand
we'll go on an adventure
because you know, you and I
we're in this together.

# IF I SAW YOU AGAIN

If I ever saw you again
would it be like all those other times
confessing our darkest secrets and hopeless fears
until we passed out way past midnight
and knowing that we'd always have each other
when nothing in life was going right
or would it be quick glances and awkward hellos
both of us desperate
to get to the other side of the road
would you do the same as I know that I would do
and watch me as I turn my back
to walk away from you.
I've been struggling to sleep
since the day you left my life
with not a single explanation
nothing to ease my mind
for some reason you decided that this was for the best
but I would jump at any given chance
to start all over again
and life has never granted me with any second chances
an opportunity to finish what I started
I know I should have told you the second I knew
that you were all I ever wanted
but if I ever saw you again
I hope to God I can find the courage
to tell you everything that's written in this poem
and if life was just like the movies
you would hold me tight and tell me
that you've always loved me
if like was like the movies
we would finally get our happy ending.

# BEAUTIFUL THINGS

I write a lot about the ugly things in life
self hatred, wars, the media
but I want to dedicate this poem
to the beautiful things
the things that too many people overlook
like the first flowers born again in Spring
waking up early and hearing the birds sing
watching the sunset on a hot Summers day
and being able to see the countryside
without buildings getting in the way.
I wish that people would stop what they're doing
and just look at the world sometimes
but everyone's too busy getting on with their life
and I hate how the human race
think that we're superior
because I believe all these things I've listed
are far more greater.

# FIND YOUR PURPOSE

I don't think we will ever understand the ways of the world
the great mysteries that have never been solved
but I feel like nobody even tries to anymore
we walk through life like robots
sleep, eat, work, repeat
tell me, where is the adventure
where is the passion
where is the desire to be more
the curiosity to know more
the courage to do what we want and say what we feel
without worrying about the consequences
because we all want to know our purpose on Earth
to know why we were created
but I think the big test in life
is simply to live
freely, carelessly, hopefully, happily
because we all have days, some of us even months
where nothing is okay
we all have times when we think to ourselves
is it really worth it
the answer is yes, absolutely
so come on, get out of your rut
open your eyes and look at the world around you
realise how beautiful it really is
read more poetry, listen to more music
fall in love, do something daring
but whatever you do
make sure it makes you feel happy
make sure it makes you feel alive
find your purpose in life.

# WRITING THE BETTER YOU BACK TO LIFE

It's time for me to accept the truth
I'll never be able to stop writing poems about you
because you walked away and left me empty
until I discovered some ink and blank pages
so I guess these poems are my way of healing
even though sometimes it doesn't seem to be working
but I will write and write
until all of this makes sense
until I can understand what was going through your head
I will write about all those good times we shared
back when you still loved me
back when you still cared
I will write about it life together growing up
back when I believed that nothing could come between us
and yes, I know
that I'll never be able to change a thing
or make you regret your reasons for leaving
I know that I won't be able
to make you come running back to me
or be able to make you see this situation the way that I see
I'm not that naïve to think
that you could ever be the same sister
who looked after me when we were kids
because I realise now that's it's all about you
do what you say, not what you do
I realise now
that you're not the person you used to be
but I can still keep that person alive in my poetry.

# WHAT HAPPENS NOW

We met, we fell in love
I used to think that was enough
but I realised I can't live off just your kiss
I deserve more out of life than this
I forgave you countless times
and gave you plenty of time to change
now I'm starting to believe
that you think this is just a game
but you only get so many lives
before it's game over
now I know that our relationship
cannot last forever
I talked, you didn't listen
same as usual
when will you ever understand
that we can't just carry on as normal?
I threw my ring across the room at you
and stormed out of the door
and I didn't come crawling back
like all those times before
you didn't run after me
haven't texted or called
and now I'm starting to wonder
if I mean anything to you at all.
I laid my cards on the table
now the ball is in your court
show me the part of you
that I stayed so long for
this is some serious stuff, not just some pretty row
we both need to decide, once and for all
what happens now.

# I WILL FORGET YOU

I have known loss and I have known pain
but I never thought I'd be the one
to call it a day
never thought I'd be in the position
of having to make the hardest decision
of either trying to mend the broken pieces
or just throwing them away
and even thought this was my choice
even though this is what I wanted
I thought that you would have at least tried to stop me
because you always said you'd never let me
get away so easily
so tell me what happened
what made you change your mind
did you suddenly decide
that we weren't worth your time
but I guess that's just the way it's always been
one of the reasons why I had to end this
because I always put my everything
into our relationship
and you contributed next to nothing
so all I can do is move on with my life
and try to forget that you're no longer mine
I will forget all those sweet words you said
all those plans we made lying in bed
to get married and have two children
plans I now realise would never have happened
and even though I lost
the one person I thought I would always want
at least I still have myself.

# THE BEST PART ABOUT ME

I met you at a point in my life
when I had lost the closest person to me
and nothing was going right
but you helped me through
and you were so nice
I thought that you entering my life
was some sort of sign
and I realise now that it was
but for different reasons
than I thought back then
because in the beginning
everything was amazing
until I discovered all your problems
when everything started changing
and I tried my best to help you through them
I know that I did
but I guess it just wasn't what you wanted.
I want you to know
that I don't hate you for that
and I could never regret what we had
because even though this love
couldn't last forever
you still gave me the courage
to make myself better
when everything was fine
it was because of you
that I wanted to make something of my life
I found the strength to do something
I never thought I'd be able to do
to love myself as much as I loved you
so now I just need to going to carry on loving myself
without you there to guide me along
because sometimes you don't need someone
to catch you when you fall
and I might not believe it now
but one day I will know it's the truth

the best part about me
is that I no longer need you.

# WISHFUL THINKING

Why can't we just forget all our worries
and say "fuck it"
throw a dart at a map
and go wherever it lands
just pack our bags
and jump on the next plane out of here
without having to worry
about how much money we haven't got
without having to think
about all the responsibilities we hide away from.

Why can't we just start over
turn the page and erase
everything we know
because we will be learning better things
wherever it is we go
we could make the world our own
and we wouldn't have to stay
in the same place for long
because for as long as I'm with you
I will always be home.

We could do whatever we wanted to do
because you know we don't have to
abide by societies rules
and doing anything would be better
than doing nothing in this one small room.

Why don't we just go on an adventure
explore the world and see the sights
figure out what it's like
to feel alive
for once
why can't we just enjoy our life.

# WHEN TRAGEDY HAPPENS

When tragedy happens
we want the world to stop
but it keeps on spinning
and life goes on
even though there are people
who just had their last breath robbed
each thought there are children
who won't get the chance to grow up.

When tragedy happens
we can only imagine the fear
the thoughts that ran through their minds
as they ran for their lives
we can only imagine what it's like
for all the families left behind.

When tragedy happens
we do all that we can
we leave flowers and our condolences
we raise awareness and cash
but there's nothing we can do
to turn back the time
nothing we do
can bring them back to life.

When tragedy happens
we remember past attacks
when they broke our hearts
but they could never break us.

# MAKING PEACE WITH YOURSELF

It won't happen instantly but gradually
like a slow burning candle
and it won't be handed to you
like the gift you've always wanted on Christmas day
you will need to work hard for it
to fight through the insecurities
that feast on your mind
telling you that you are not worthy
you will need to break down the walls
that stop you from letting yourself in
that stop you from accepting yourself
I know you think that this is impossible
and you know as well as anyone
that nothing in life comes easy
but that doesn't mean that you stop trying
so take a deep breath or maybe two
let the bad thoughts wash over you
like the roaring waves as the tide comes in
say to yourself that you don't need to be perfect
and it's okay to make mistakes
keep repeating this until you believe it
because one day you wipe off the debris
and destruction that hating yourself created
and you will stand up tall in the midst of it all
and realise
that all those years you were at war with yourself
were never peaceful
and the next time you prepare to go into battle
you will remind yourself
that it's not wars that make peace
but people.

# BLANK PAGE

Our lives start out as a blank page
there to ink all of our adventures upon
whether good or downright terrible
but there have been plenty of times
when I wished I had written my life in pencil
so that I could erase all my bad moments and mistakes
there have been times I wished I could forget everything
and start from the very beginning
but I have since realised
that our lives are not supposed to be perfect
we are supposed to experience heartbreak and pain
and what it feels like to feel
so small in this gigantic world
because with mistakes and pain comes wisdom
we need them to help us grow
and life is not just a never-ending circle of misery
in between the bad moments
we are rewarded by incredible ones
like first kisses and last dances
and anything else that might make us happy
I guess what I'm trying to say
is that we shouldn't worry too much
about making every moment perfect
because the book titled life is a long one
and it's not yet published
so there's plenty of time to edit it.

# THE THING I LOVE THE MOST

I love words
because they can be used to create stories
to transport you to other worlds
they can be used to motivate you, inspire you
and to pick you back up
when you've been left in the dirt
but words can also be the reason why
you were left in the dirt in the first place
people can use words to hurt you
and discriminate you
because of your gender, sexuality or race
and it's always the hurtful words
that stick in our minds
no matter how hard I've tried
there are things that have been said to me
that have torn me apart
and I hate how the thing that I love the most
has the power to break my heart.

# WOULDN'T IT BE GREAT

Wouldn't it be great if all pain was visible
so that everyone could see
exactly what you were going through
you wouldn't have to lie and say "I'm okay"
because everyone would know that wasn't the case.

Wouldn't it be great if everyone was understanding
and you knew it would be alright
if you wanted to speak to someone
about what was going on in your life.

Wouldn't it be great
if people didn't judge
if we could all live our own lives
and have that be enough
because at the end of the day
we all process pain
in completely different ways
no matter how big or small
even if it doesn't seem like a great big deal at all
nobody has the right to say
that somebody else has it worse
nobody has the right to make you feel guilty
for being hurt.

# DEBRIS

You found me lying in the debris
of my broken heart
but you gave me your hand and helped me up
you made me believe in love
I thought that all we would be
is passing ships in the night
but you have been there for me
ever since that night
now those moments of being afraid, desperate and lonely
are locked safely away
at the very back of my memory
and even if they sometimes manage to creep
to the forefront of my mind
I know that you are always there
to kiss away the nightmares
and tell me that everything is going to be okay
I know that you are always
just a phone call away
and you will always listen to whatever I have to say
and what I want to say right now is "thank you"
because you found me lying in the debris
of my broken heart
you made me believe that life can restart.

# STANDING ALONE IN A CROWDED ROOM

It's been four years since we parted ways
and I still haven't got back that part of myself
that I liked the best
and I have no idea what happened
don't know where it all went wrong
but I didn't realise just how much I needed you
until you were gone
didn't realise I didn't have a voice
until you stopped singing the song
and I've tried turning strangers into my home
but your shelter is all I've ever known
I've tried having the confidence to follow my arrow
but how can I do that
when I've always just been your shadow?
Loneliness is a word I was always foreign you
because at the end of the day
I always had you
but I stood by as your burned all your bridges
I watch our entire life together go up in smoke
now even in a crowded room, I feel so alone
and I have no idea how to change this
I don't know how to fill this emptiness in my chest
when just being your sister
is what I've always done best.

# YOU'RE STILL ON MY MIND

It's 2am and I'm struggling to sleep
because whenever something was on my mind
you were always there to listen to me
but you're gone now
like you were never even here
and I really try to stop myself
but I still think about you, my dear
I think about what never was
and what could have been
I think about what could have happened
if you'd had the same feelings as me
and I'm listening to that song
that we used to sing together
back when we were good
and back when life was better
it got me thinking
about the way we were before
and even though you were never mine
may I say I loved you more?

# THE OTHER PART OF ME

When you left
a part of me left with you
and the part that remains
is just trying to make it through
through the loss, the pain
through the wishing you were here
to get me through the darkest days
I hope the other part of me
is doing well
and that she still has you to hold her up
whenever the world
comes crashing down around her
whenever she feels like
she'll never be strong enough
I hope you haven't abandoned her
just like you abandoned me
that she isn't wandering around all alone
on the corner of the street
but in all honesty
I hope the other part of me
never made her way to you
because I know that inevitably
you will leave her too.

# EVERYTHING TO ME

People say that life is too short
but I would happily spend eternity
here in this bed with you
studying your every nook and cranny
and kissing you passionately
in between listening to your stories
and I've got poem after poem
written down in notebooks
describing all the reasons why I love you
because just saying those words is not enough
just saying "I love you"
is too simple to describe how I feel
you are, to me
the last drop of water in the sea
that moment when you listen to a song
for the very first time
and realise how much you need it in your life
you are the motivation
that gets me up in the morning
the realisation that maybe
this day, this month, this life
will not be too daunting
you are the transition
from rain to sunshine
the good news you desperately need
when nothing in life is going right
I would tell you all this if I had the nerve
but you and I know
that I'm only good at writing words
so know that when I say "I love you"
it's not lightly
because it's written in all my poems
that you are everything to me.

# DEAR BODY

I am sorry
for not taking better care of you
and for not loving you
as much as I should
I am sorry for listening to them
when they said you're not worthy of love
I am sorry
for all those times
I stood in front of the mirror
wishing you were taller, prettier, thinner
I am sorry
for making all those marks
that can never be erased
and for all those times
I just wanted you to disappear
I am sorry
for being ashamed
for the longest time
I believed that I
was defined by the way I look
and to the rest of the world
it was never good enough
but I realise now
that there are more important things
than the colour of your hair
or the size of your jeans
and I'm sorry
for all those flaws
that I tried my best to hide
I know now that true beauty
lies on the inside
I am sorry
for hating you so much
and for all those years of neglect
dear body, I am sorry
for expecting you to be perfect.

# I ALREADY MISS YOU

Sometimes I miss you
even though you're right beside me
and sometimes I feel so lonely
even though you're always there for me
you see
there's a gaping hole inside my chest
the effect of everyone
who entered my life
and then left
so I guess I'm mentally preparing myself
for when your turn comes
for the day when you decide
that you've finally had enough
and walk right out the door
because it's inevitable
I know that it is
I guess I'm not the kind of person
you can love for eternity
and everyone knows that nothing lasts forever
not even our love
that we have worked so hard at to put back together
so I'm trying to cherish the good times now
whilst we still have them
I'm trying to stop thinking about the future
and trying to live in the moment
but despite how positive I try to be
I know what will eventually happen
there's nothing either of us will be able to do
and the day might be a long time coming
but I already miss you.

# A GOOD LIFE

Once in a while, I like to stop
and take a look around at the world
to admire the beauty that we still have left
I like to take a moment to remind myself
just how much I am blessed
because we don't need
any of these material things in life, that we all crave
money, houses, fancy cars
all of these will eventually go away
it's the little things that make life worthwhile
sunsets, new years and warm, friendly smiles
the feeling of happiness and being in love
this is what a good life is made of
so I don't care if I end up with no money
because I can't take it wherever I'll finally be going
if I smile often and laugh a lot
it doesn't matter what else I haven't got
because that is more than enough
to make me happy.

# TODAY

I find it strange
that all around the world
everyone is experiencing today
in a completely different way
someone is falling in love
for the first time
whilst somebody else's heart is breaking
someone is crying themselves to sleep at night
whilst somebody else is having the time of their life
someone is just being born
whilst somebody else is taking their last breath
but what I think is wonderful
is that we all have the same feelings
we all, sooner or later
go through the same things
so if you're feeling lonely tonight
like you're the only man on the moon
if you're thinking that there's no way
anyone understands what you're going through
trust me, they do
I want you to know that you're never alone
no matter how many times it feels like you are
and I want you to remember
that you will not feel this way forever
billions of people
have survived everything you have been through
so take that as proof
that no matter what gets thrown your way
you will always make it through today.

## INSPIRE ME

Tell me stories about your childhood
and all that you hold close to your heart
trust ne with your most haunting secret
the one you can't tell even yourself
and be patient with me
whilst I gather up the courage to tell you mine
kiss me on the couch
and tell me how pretty I am
again and again until I believe you
lay with me in these bed sheets
and caress my body with your fingertips
despite my lack of self-esteem
help me figure out the meaning
behind the wretched look in my eyes
and be my reason for happiness
make me fall in love with you
like I could never fall in love with the world
and as my pen hovers over this empty page
give me something beautiful to write about
inspire me.

# IN A PERFECT WORLD

In a perfect world
war wouldn't exist
we would settle our differences
over long conversations, tea and biscuits
in a perfect world
there would be no bombings
no kidnapping, murdering or mass shootings
nobody would be bullied
discriminated against or segregated
everything that is now corrupt
would be eradicated
there would be no evil
in a perfect world
we would all love one another
and not just only
after thousands have been killed.

But this is the world we live
and it's the only one we're going to get
but I haven't lost my faith
in humanity yet
the power to change the future
is in our hands
I know it would take a lot time
and the world could never be perfect
but if we could prevent
even the tiniest even
wouldn't it be worth it?

# TRANSFORMED

It is said that every seven years your body changes
that every cell is replaced
and you are transformed into a complete new person
if that's true
I hope that next time
you transform back to the person you used to be
because I don't recognise you anymore
I find myself delving into our memories together
in an effort to keep the old you alive
you were the person I could always turn to
no matter what
the person I could always tell my secrets to
but now all my secrets are the bad habits I've fallen into
trying to forget what you have turned in to
you are the monster I feared was under my bed
when I was a little girl
and the beautiful Queen
who turned out to be a witch
when we were younger
I thought you were my hero
now all that I can think is
you're not the person I grew up with
and I wish that our feelings
get replaced every seven years too
because I still miss you.

# I'LL NEVER FORGET US

I'll never forget
those first few months of our life
when everything was magical
and everything felt right
kissing in the rain, feeling safe in your arms
gazing at the stars on blankets in my backyard.

I'll never forget
how you said we were meant to be
I'll never forget all my anxieties
or all those silent tears I shed
whilst you were lying next to me
fast asleep in bed
you played the part of the perfect boyfriend
it took me so long to realise
that it was all just pretend.

I'll never forget
all those plans we discussed
and how they all just turned into dust
I used to think you were a hopeless romantic
now I realise that you're just hopeless
all that time I spent trying to build a life for us
and you thought that only your words would be enough.

I'll never forget the silence that followed
when I said I don't want to be with you anymore
the words I'd been dying to say for years
made my heart sink to the floor
but when all is said and all is done
I don't know why I spent so long holding on.

Now that it's over
I can finally breathe
because I'll never forget
how it felt like you were suffocating me

now that I've finally lifted the anchor
and set us both free
I can start to remember what I loved about my life
before it was just you and I.

# I MISS YOU

I miss you
like a toothache
you were a pain
that I got used to.

# THAT'S LIFE

The only thing
in life that's inevitable
is death
yet we hide from it
like shadows afraid of the dark
we believe in silly superstitions
because burying pieces of a shattered mirror
or throwing salt over our shoulders
isn't as bad as knowing that one day
this will all be over
but we don't know when and we don't know how
we're just told how to live in the here and now
don't smoke, don't drink
don't do anything that can cause cancer
and every day the list gets longer
get a job so don't become homeless and hungry
but you could still lose it all
after helping win the fight for your country
believe in God and you'll earn a place in Heaven
even thought nobody knows if that will really happen
look after your health and everything will be fine
but nobody knows how they're going to die
I know it's important to look after yourself
to try and live as long as we can
in the only life that we get
but sometimes I think we forget we're actually alive
and instead of living, we only survive
I'm guilty of this too
I know that I am
I'm caught in the trap as much as anyone
but I want to break free from the boxes
that the world slots us in
the world that tells us how to do everything
I like my life
I like it just fine
I just want to make sure

that my life is actually mine.

## OUR WORLD

We had the world in the palm of our hands
it used to revolve around just us
and nothing or no-one could tear us down
until I broke down these walls
I had been hiding behind.

I used to think you were all I wanted
that everything else would just fall into place
that as long as I had you
life would be perfect
but perfect doesn't exist
and everyone makes mistakes.

It used to be you and me
against the world
now it's just me
for the world
because the world is a wonderful place to be
a place I've always wanted to see.

# HOW DO I LET GO

I wear my heart upon my sleeve
and I see the best in everyone I meet
but the people who mean the most to me
always end up in my history
please tell me, how do I let go?

I have a few close friends who I adore
who I know will be there for me forevermore
yet I can't help but feel alone
even surrounded by people who feel like home
because I can't help but think about
all the people I used to know
please tell me, how do I let go?

I've come a long way from the girl I used to be
the girls with a heavy heart
and a mountain of insecurities
but something will happen that stops me in my tracks
a melancholy memory that takes me right back
and I know that the past
is supposed to stay in the past
but won't someone please
please tell me, how do I let go?

# OUR KALEIDOSCOPE KINGDOM

Everything was smoke and mirrors
when I thought that I was happy
I was just caught up in the moment
our love was an illusion
and we had everyone under our spell
even I still believed in your magic
back when we first met
believed that you could wave a wand
and make all my problems seem small

The curse was lifted a long time ago
but like I was wrapped I'm invisible chains
I just couldn't let you go
I was too scared to give up
the life I'd been building with you for so long
but I saw our world through a kaleidoscope
and knew that things had to change
I couldn't carry on living my life this way.

Now looking back on our history
I realise that it was all down to me
I gave you seven years of my life
but now I'm ready to take what was always mine
because I built our empire all on my own
now it's time for me to claim my throne.

# WHEN I THINK ABOUT THE WORLD

When I think about the world
it makes me want to cry
for all the homeless people
we pretend we didn't see
out of the corner of our eye
for the neglected children and the outcasts
and the people who believe
that they have nothing to do with any of that
for everyone who is silently suffering
terrified and confused
for everyone who feels like
they have nobody to turn to
and I can't help but feel at fault
I wish I could just wave a magic wand
and correct all of the worlds wrongs
but mostly I wish
that I could tap into the minds
of people who don't care about any of this at all
of people who always have better things to do
than to stop and listen
to what other people are going through
and of people who are the cause
behind the effect
the reason why these people
are broken and wrecked
because I want to know why
these people can destroy
another human being and think that's fine
I want to know why
for us to care about one another
it takes having to die
why can't we all stand together
whilst we're still alive
I've been wondering if it's ever going to stop
all this senseless hatred that's been going on

for centuries too long
and it's alright saying
"I need to put myself first"
but I'm sure you've needed help
when you were at your worst
why is it so hard for us
to show basic human compassion
and lend a helping hand
I wonder how long it's going to take
for us to learn how to love
and forget how to hate.

# LIFE WITHOUT YOU

Even though I'm getting my life on track
part of me feels like I've taken a step back
part of me wants to swallow my pride
and run back to your place
with my arms open wide
because it feels strange no longer hearing your voice
even thought I used to hate the noise
it feels strange no longer holding you
even though it's what I never wanted to do
they say you don't know what you've got
until it's gone
I knew exactly what I had
and it was all wrong
you weren't right for me
but I held on for too long
and now I'm facing the reality
of a life I threw you out of.

# IF I'M BEING HONEST

If I'm being honest with myself
whatever we had wasn't love
just memories of being caught up in the moment
and a lifetime of thinking
that without you I'd be homeless
but I've learnt
that you can't use people as shelter
because sooner or later
their cracks will start to show
yet you stay
because for the longest time
they were all you've ever known.

You think that you tried your best
but it was not nearly enough
and I've been battling with my emotions
for so many years
emptied myself out
after all these wasted tears
I used to think
that we'd get our happily ever after
but truth be told
we never had a future
and if I'm being honest with myself
our past is already out of view
if I'm being honest with myself
it's not me, it's you.

# I AM JUST A GIRL

If I were a pen
I would have the neatest writing
there's no room for mistakes
on the paper that I'm using

If I were a bird
I would fly beyond the clouds
what's the use of having wings
if you just stay on the ground

If I were the ocean
I would wash my fears away
start all over again
as if there were never any debris

But I am just a girl
and I don't know what to do
in a word
that only tells me what not to.

# HAPPY ON MY OWN

You can learn a lot about yourself
by being on your own
such as realising that doesn't mean
that you're alone
I've gained a new perspective
since I kicked you out of my life
a life that finally feels like mine
because now I'm doing
what I've always wanted to do
which is everything
just not with you
I've learnt to stop apologising
for putting myself first
when I'm the most important person
in my world
you can say that I need somebody else
but I'm stress-free and happy by myself
you can tell me I can't do this on my own
but I'm a motherfucking Queen
just let me sit on my throne.

# THE NEXT TIME I FALL IN LOVE

When we met
it felt like I'd known you my whole life
now seven years later
we're strangers again
and even thought it was my call
I sometimes forget
that you're no longer mine
I guess you can get used to anything
that's a part of your life for so long
I flashback to times
when you made me feel happy
to times when it felt like the world
was built for you just you and I
I sometimes still wish
that it wasn't all just a distant memory
but I can't change my feelings
or the past
and honestly, if I could
I don't think I would
because we were long past our expiration date
so now it's time to move on
but I could never regret loving you
I'll cherish all those moments we shared
as everything we experience in life
is a learning curve
so now I know what to not to do
the next time I fall in love.

# FREEDOM FROM YOU

I never thought that freedom from you
would feel so good
never thought I'd be able to breathe so easily
without having you around me
and all those moments we shared
I don't even miss
between not one thing about you
is amazing as this
this euphoria I've been living in
ever since I ended things
for the first time in a long time
I am happy with my life
I'm no longer panicking
that I'm running out of time
because now I only have myself to think about
and I control my own future
who knows where I'd be now
if I had realised this sooner.

# WHEN HISTORY IS FORGOTTEN

When people are at war with themselves
and the rest don't care
about caring for others
where do you turn for help
when everything is kept under the covers.

When those with the power to change things
are those making sure they stay the same
how are you supposed to win
when you're not in a position to play the game.

When history is forgotten
and shots keep being fired
when we still live in a world
where people just refuse to listen
and you're scared that the present
is looking a lot like the past
turn towards the future
and fight until you have surpassed
fight for a time
when peace on Earth isn't only a dream
and when everybody has the right to be free.

# IN THE SPACES BETWEEN THE SHADOWS

Everywhere I turn
I see death and destruction
I turn on the news
to see another country has been tortured
I see people turning a blind eye
to the horrors of the world
as they go about their normal
every day lives
but on the flipside
I see thousands of people
praying for those who have died
I see hope in the eyes
of those who care
and those who have survived
seeing all of this makes me realise
that good and evil
can exist at the same time
because between shades of grey
there is white
and in the spaces between the shadows
there is light.

## ABOUT THE AUTHOR

Laura Harrison is an ordinary 25-year-old living in Manchester, England with her parents and dogs.

She started writing poetry in 2012 in an attempt to make sense of the world and her feelings.

When she isn't writing, she can always be found with her nose in a young adult novel.

In the Spaces Between the Shadows is her first collection of poetry.

Printed in Great Britain
by Amazon

35714264R00038